HAL LEONARD UKULELE METHOD BOOK 2

BY LIL' REV

ISBN 978-1-4234-1617-3

HAL•LEONARD®
CORPORATION
7777 W. BLUEMOUND RD. P.O. BOX 13819 MILWAUKEE, WI 53213

Copyright © 2008 by HAL LEONARD CORPORATION
International Copyright Secured   All Rights Reserved

In Australia Contact:
Hal Leonard Australia Pty. Ltd.
4 Lentara Court
Cheltenham, Victoria, 3192 Australia
Email: ausadmin@halleonard.com.au

Visit Hal Leonard Online at
www.halleonard.com

INTRODUCTION

Welcome to the Hal Leonard *Ukulele Method Book 2*. This follow-up to *Book 1* emphasizes both melody playing and related right-hand techniques. After having completed the first book, you should now possess an understanding of how to tune the ukulele, basic notation and tab reading, basic chords in the keys of C, F, G, E minor and D minor, simple melody playing, 3/4 time, the single-roll stroke, and a growing repertoire of some standard melodies.

To build on this knowledge, *Book 2* will carry you further into the wonderful world of *uke-dom* by helping to expand your chord and scale vocabulary. I'll teach you many new right-hand techniques, including the five-finger roll, ragtime strum, calypso strum, and the much-revered triplet stroke, along with new chords, and hammer-ons and pull-offs for the fretting hand.

We'll also learn about diminished and movable chords, how to play a boogie-woogie, Tin Pan Alley songs, dotted quarter notes, and 6/8 time, along with minor keys, 3/4 time, and much, much more.

As always, have fun! Practice and soon you'll have everyone singing—and smiling—with your love of the uke!

Aloha,

—Lil' Rev

ABOUT THE AUTHOR

Lil' Rev is a Milwaukee, Wisconsin-based award-winning multi-instrumentalist, writer, photographer, and music historian. He tours the U.S. teaching and performing original and traditional folk, blues, ethnic, and old-time music. To learn more about Lil' Rev's schedule, recordings, or programs, visit *www.lilrev.com*.

Special thanks to Jennifer Rupp.

Thanks to Will Branch for technical assistance.

THE KEY OF D

The key of D has two sharped notes: F sharp and C sharp. The diagram shows where these notes appear on the fretboard next to their neighboring natural notes.

Reminder: The sharp symbol (#) raises a note by one half step and the flat symbol (♭) lowers a note by one half step.

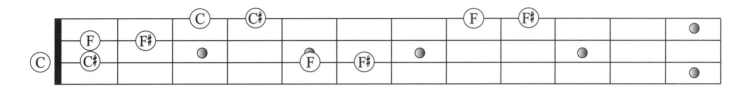

Here's where the new notes appear on the musical staff.

We'll begin with a D major scale. Play this slowly, one note for each foot tap.

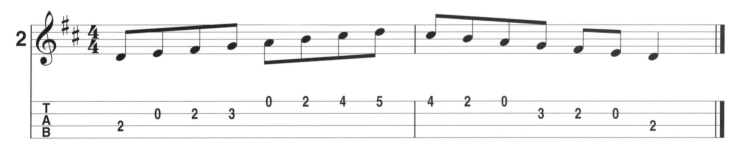

Now let's try it in eighth notes. Remember, one quarter note equals two eighth notes, so play two notes for each tap of the foot here. Also notice that the top note of the scale is not repeated this time, so that the last note comes out on beat 4.

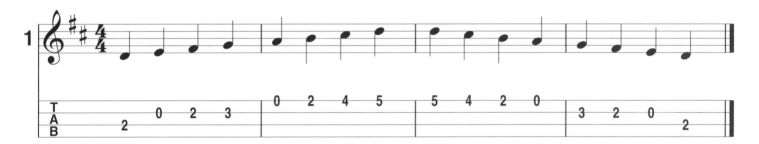

Good. Now, let's try a very simple melody from Pachelbel's "Canon in D." Nothing but half notes here. Each note lasts for two beats. Don't rush!

KEY OF D EXERCISES

Great! Now, let's play something that moves around a bit. Be careful and play this slowly at first. Watch how it leaps from string to string.

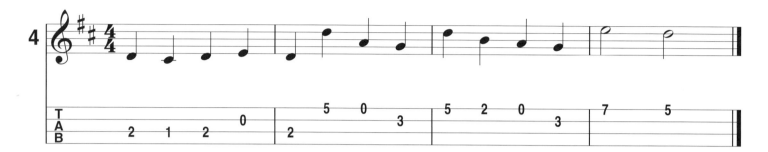

A simple nursery song, yes, but watch out for the rests and the eighth notes.

REPEATS

Repeat signs tell you to repeat everything that is between them. Play through the section once until you hit the second repeat sign (:|), then go back to the first repeat sign (|:), play the section again, and continue to the end.

Let's play the D major scale again, this time using two eighth notes per pitch. Notice the repeat signs in this example. Play through the whole thing twice.

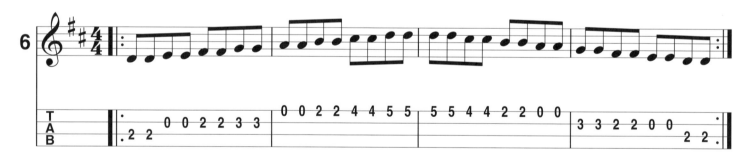

Start slowly with this melodic exercise, practicing it again and again until you can play it fast and smooth.

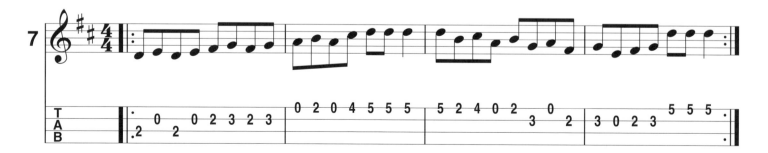

THE D CHORD FAMILY
D, D7, G, G7, and A7 Chords

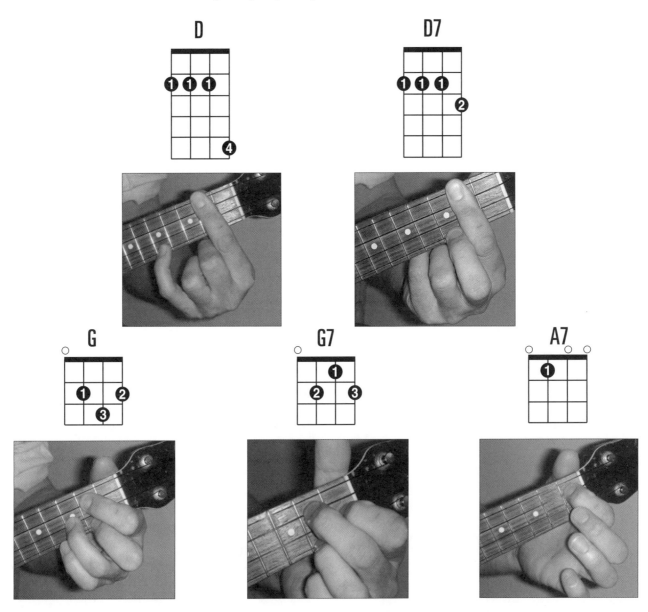

First, practice finding the chords above. Then say the name of each chord aloud as you practice these exercises, strumming slowly.

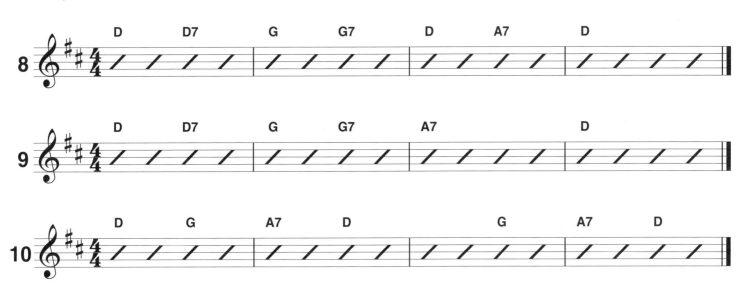

Let's go back and add a C chord!

STRUM-ALONG TUNES IN D

Here is a medley of some fun tunes using the new D, G, and A7 chords. Play these songs at your own speed so you can hit the chord changes on time. Count "1, 2, 3, 4," putting the emphasis on 2 and 4 as you strum.

In the chord diagrams the letters *fr* refer to the fret position of your first (index) finger when playing the chord.

STAGOLEE

Blues Folk Song

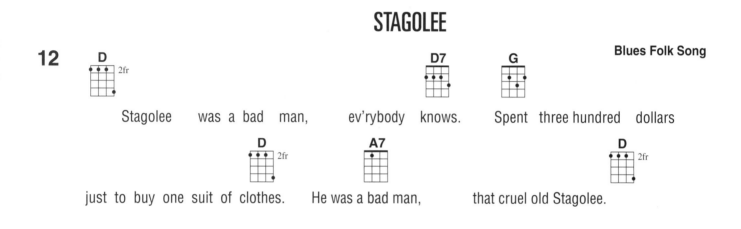

THE OLD CHISHOLM TRAIL

Traditional Cowboy Song

6

HEY LOLLY, LOLLY

Calypso

14

 D

A7

Married man's an easy rider, hey lolly, lolly low. Single boy gets

D

all excited, hey lolly, lolly low. Hey, lolly, lolly, lolly, hey, lolly,

A7

D

lolly low. Hey lolly, lolly, lolly, hey, lolly, lolly low.

D MAJOR READING

Here is our first melody in the key of D. Remember to follow the key signature and play all the F notes as F#'s (and all the C's as C#'s, though none come up in this tune).

This tune has some **dotted half notes**. As we learned in *Book 1*, a dot after a note increases its beat value by one half. Since a half note is two beats long, a dotted half note is three beats long.

LIL' LIZA JANE

Classic American Folk

15

1. I know a gal that I a-dore, lil' Li - za Jane. Way down south in
2. Down where she lives the po-sies grow, lil' Li - za Jane. Chick-ens 'round the

Bal - ti - more, lil' Li - za Jane.
kitch - en door, lil' Li - za Jane.

Oh, E - li - za, lil' Li - za

Jane. Oh, E - li - za, lil' Li - za Jane.

7

DOTTED QUARTER NOTES

You already know that a dot after a note increases its value by one half. The next tune contains **dotted quarter notes**. Since a quarter note equals one beat, a dotted quarter note equals one and a half beats. Count "1 and 2" for the A note in the melody (on the word "row"). Then the next note, F♯, starts on the "and" of beat 2.

ENDINGS

The following song has a first and second ending indicated by brackets with the numbers 1 and 2.

When you reach the repeat sign (:‖) in the first ending, go back to the first repeat sign (‖:). On the second time through, skip the first ending and go on to the second ending.

Gray chord symbols are used in the next tune to indicate chords that back up your melody—they can be played by another uke or any other chordal instrument like a guitar or piano.

MICHAEL ROW THE BOAT ASHORE

Work Song/Spiritual

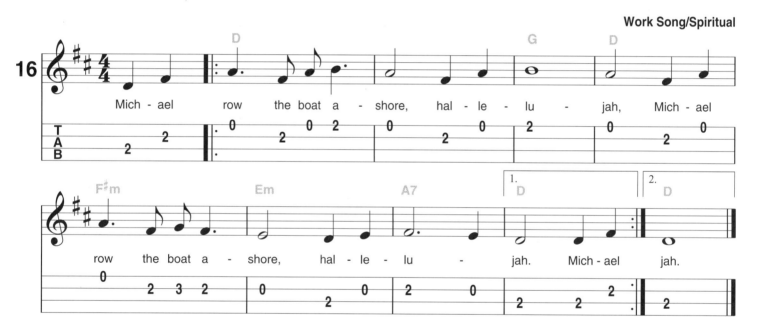

This is a classic melody that every uke player should know. It has a pickup measure that starts on an "and." Count "1 and 2 and 3" then start playing at "and 4 and." Watch for the dotted quarter notes, too!

WHEN THE SAINTS GO MARCHING IN

Gospel Hymn

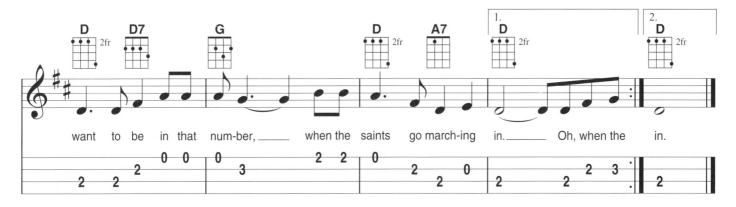

Let's take everything we have learned and try this catchy little tune. Take note of the dotted half notes, dotted quarter notes, and the eighth notes. Now you're really playing some good music!

CAMPTOWN RACES

By Stephen Foster

MOVABLE CHORDS

One of the fastest and easiest ways to expand your chordal knowledge is to use chord shapes that can be moved up and down the fretboard. This principle applies to any chord that contains no unfretted strings. We call these **closed** chord shapes.

Unlike open chords (take the open C for example), once you learn a closed chord shape, you can play many different chords by moving up and down the neck without changing your fingering.

Below you will find the three most common movable chord shapes. The shape names are based on the chords they make when played at or near the lowest position. Other players and books may use slightly varying names for the basic shapes, but the results are the same: lots of new chords produced by moving the same fingering back and forth!

Practice them up and down the neck, saying their names as you play each one. Over time and with practice, these chord shapes and positions will come very naturally to you without having to think very much about them. In the process, your playing will sound more varied and alive.

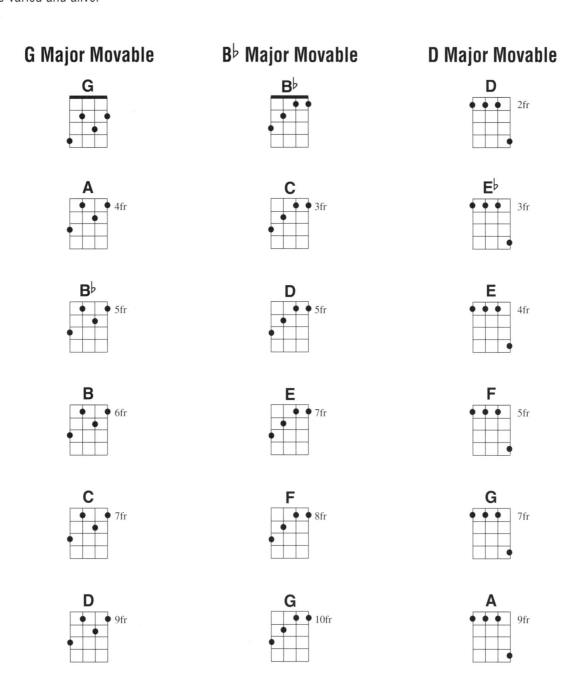

Do not pass go! Do not collect $200! Go back to the top and run through these diagrams at least 100 times or until you have their names and shapes memorized.

THE KEY OF B♭

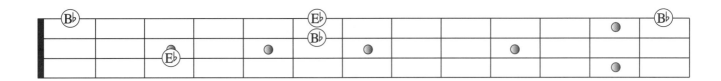

The key of B♭ has a B♭ and an E♭. All B's and E's should be played one half step (one fret) lower.

Here's where they appear on the staff:

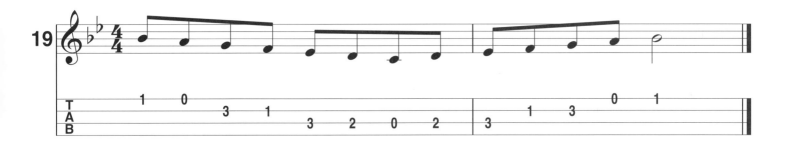

Ok! Here is a first-position B♭ major scale.

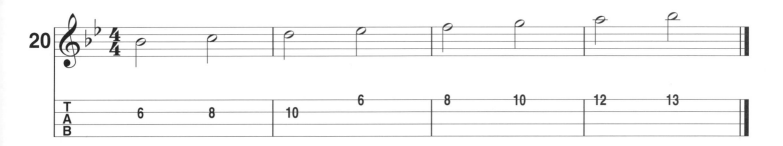

Let's move up the neck. Play the scale in nice, slow half notes first as you get used to it; one note every two beats.

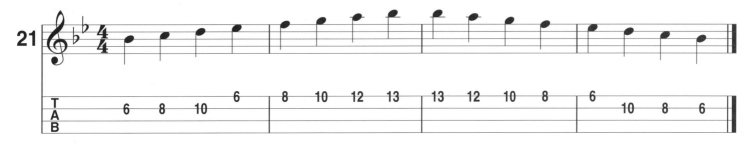

Now, up and down the scale in quarter notes; one note per beat.

THE B♭ CHORD FAMILY
B♭, B♭7, E♭, E♭7, and F7 Chords

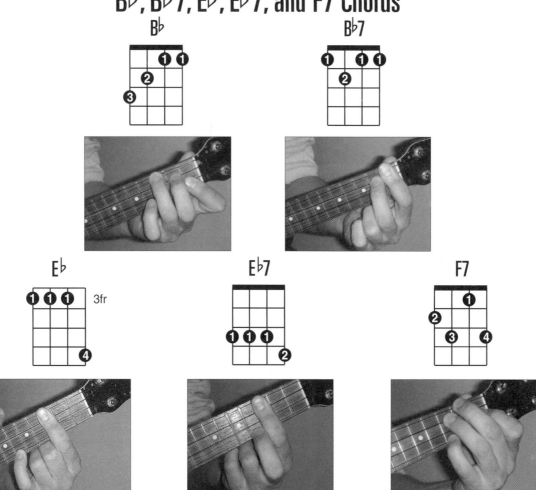

B♭ is a great key for the ukulele. Begin as you did in the key of D by fingering these chord shapes and saying their names aloud. Then practice the following three exercises.

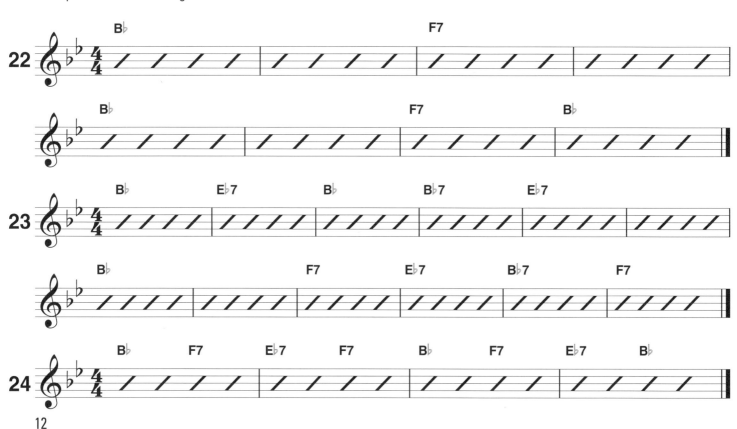

STRUM-ALONG TUNES IN B♭

Use the common stroke (down, up, down, up), emphasizing the 2nd and 4th beats of each measure, counting 1 & **2** & 3 & **4**.

ALL NIGHT LONG

Early Blues

25

Baby, all night long, baby, all night long. Oh, from midnight on, baby, all night long.

Well, I may be young, and foolish too! But I left my home on account of you.

On account of you, on account of you, well, I left my home on account of you.

THIS LITTLE LIGHT OF MINE

African American Spiritual

26

This little light of mine, I'm gonna let it shine. This little light of mine, I'm gonna let it shine.

This little light of mine, I'm gonna let it shine. Let it shine, let it shine, let it shine.

WE SHALL NOT BE MOVED

Protest Song

27

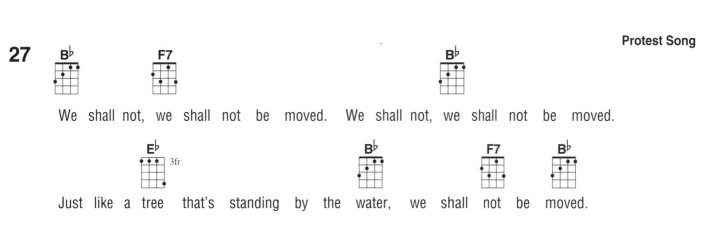

We shall not, we shall not be moved. We shall not, we shall not be moved.

Just like a tree that's standing by the water, we shall not be moved.

Now try out this melody in B♭.

GREAT SPECKLED BIRD

Arranged by Lil' Rev

3. When He cometh descending from heaven
   On the cloud that He writes in His word,
   I'll be joyfully carried to meet Him
   On the wings of that great speckled bird.

Challenge yourself with this piece. Once you have learned to play it as written, go back and try executing the four-finger roll (from *Book 1*) each time you play the B♭ and F7 chords. Another good idea is to play the chord progression using tremolo (also covered in *Book 1*) .

CARELESS LOVE

American Folk Song

3. Once I wore my apron high, (3x)
   Now I wish that man would die.

4. How I wish that train would come, (3x)
   Carry me back where I come from.

5. You see what careless love will do, (3x)
   Make you leave your mama and papa, too.

Now let's check out some tunes in different keys. Count three beats for the dotted half notes in this American classic. Remember to count through the quarter rests between the verses.

I'M A YANKEE DOODLE DANDY

By George M. Cohan

THE GOLDEN ERA OF UKULELE

Broadway and vaudeville show tunes represent a golden era of song and style. During this fertile period of early American music, the ukulele became a popular instrument. Performers Roy Smeck, Johnny Marvin, Wendell Hall, Cliff Edwards, Ukulele Bailey, and King Benny Nawahi of Hawaii soon made the uke a household staple. Sheet music for tunes like "Ain't She Sweet" and "Five Foot Two" contained ukulele chord charts that allowed everyday people to pick up the music and strum along! Songwriters like Irving Berlin and George Gershwin and singing stars like Al Jolson and Sophie Tucker would all become synonymous with what came to be known as the Tin Pan Alley Era (1892–1950), and while the names of these people may be lost to the public today, the songs they gave us and the era's main instrument—the ukulele—will live on forever.

This tune in 3/4 time is also known as "Daisy, Daisy" or "A Bicycle Built for Two." It was a top ten hit in 1893 for singer Dan Quinn. You learned about 3/4 time in *Book 1*. There are three beats per measure and the quarter note gets the beat.

DAISY BELL

By Harry Dacre

DIMINISHED SEVENTH CHORDS

A diminished seventh chord is like a minor chord except it has a lowered fifth and an added diminished (double-flatted) seventh. The chord is spelled numerically as 1–♭3–♭5–♭♭7. For example, an Adim7 chord has the notes A–C–E♭–G♭. (The natural or major 7th of A is G♯. Lowering it once gives us a G. Lowering it again gives us G♭.)

Diminished seventh chords (and three-note diminished triads, spelled 1–♭3–♭5) are often described as ominous or eerie-sounding. When instructing students in the use of diminished chords, Hawaii's foremost ukulele teacher Roy Sakuma says, "Be careful with this one. It is unstable!" He is right. When well-placed, the chord adds a special flair to blues, jazz, and ragtime styles—to name a few—but diminished chords are not to be overdone.

Watch for the letters "dim" or the small "∘" which is also used to indicate a diminished chord, especially when playing Tin Pan Alley tunes from the twenties and thirties. Sometimes the number 7 is left off the name, but that's usually the chord type that is implied.

Movable Diminished 7th Shape
You can move this one up the neck!

Open C♯∘7
This one you can't move!

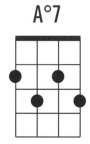

DIMINISHED EXERCISES

Now let's try a bluesy chord progression with a C♯∘7 chord added.

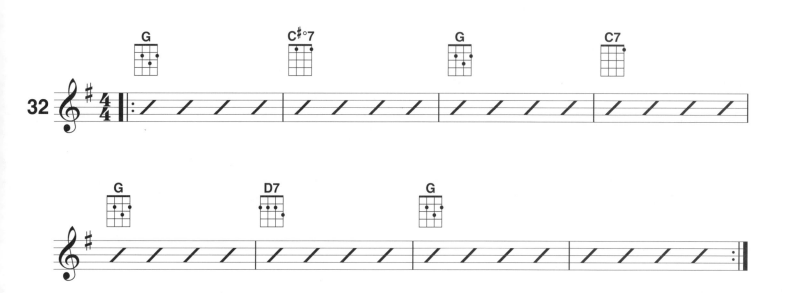

Here's a little progression reminiscent of the Tin Pan Alley era.

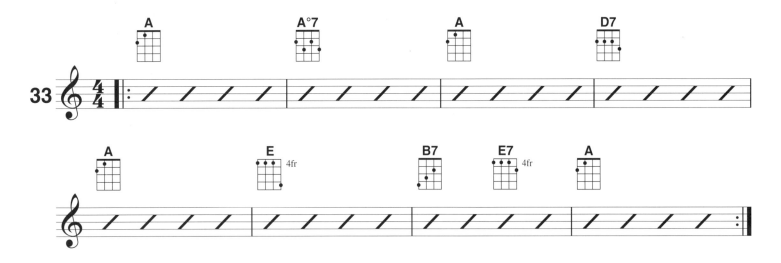

Now try this folksy use of the diminished chord.

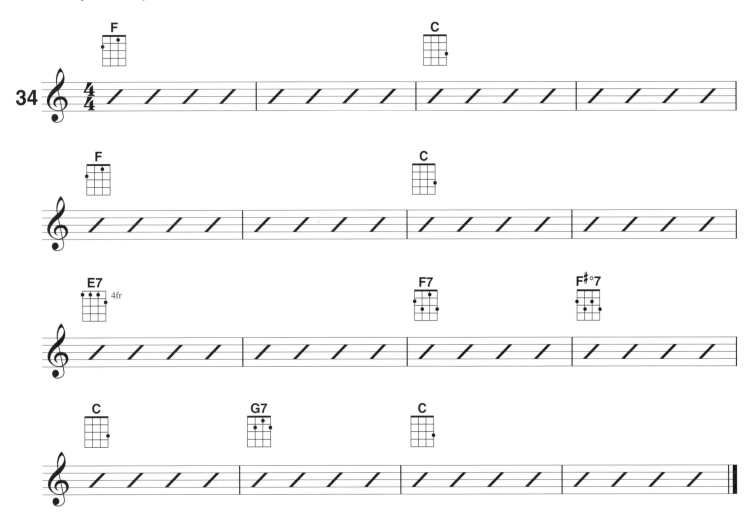

THE KEY OF A

The key of A has three sharp notes: F#, C# and G#. The neck diagram shows all three with their neighboring natural tones. Only the G# is new for us.

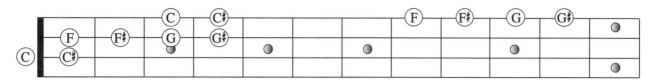

As a reminder, here are all three sharp notes we know as they appear on the staff.

This example uses the notes we can reach from the A major scale in open position. Play this using your thumb.

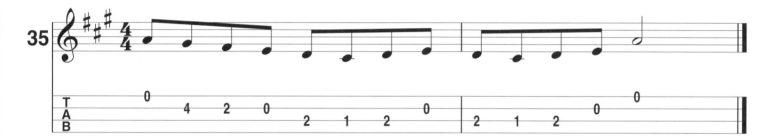

Here is a basic A major scale ascending and descending the top string only. This one will require all four fingers.

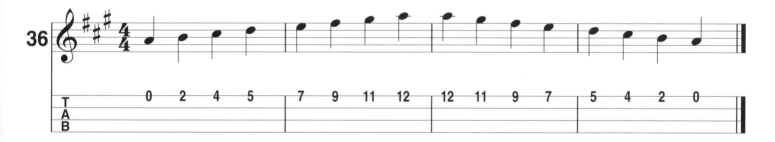

RIFFING ON SOME SHARPS

A **riff** is a short phrase that can be applied to many different kinds of tunes.

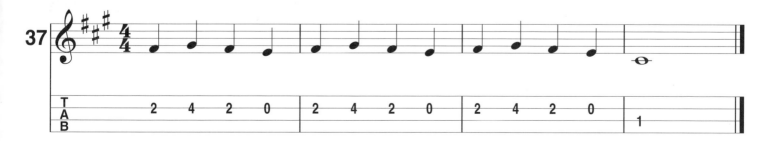

THE A CHORD FAMILY
A, D7, and E7 Chords

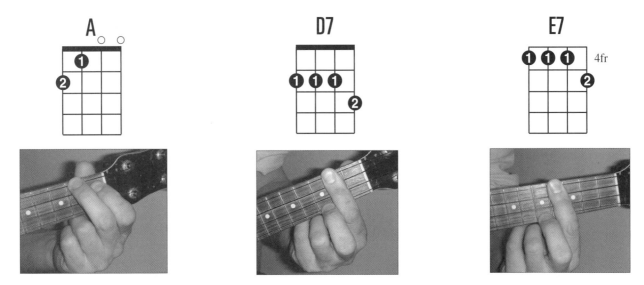

By now you should feel pretty confident about your ability to switch chords without breaking your timing. Let's play this example with this basic pattern: count "**1** and 2 and **3** and 4 and," putting the emphasis on the beats **1** and **3**.

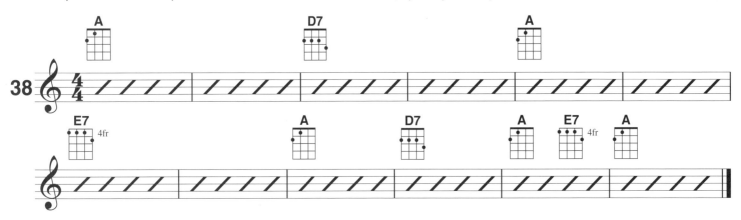

Now try the same accent pattern on these bluegrass-style progressions.

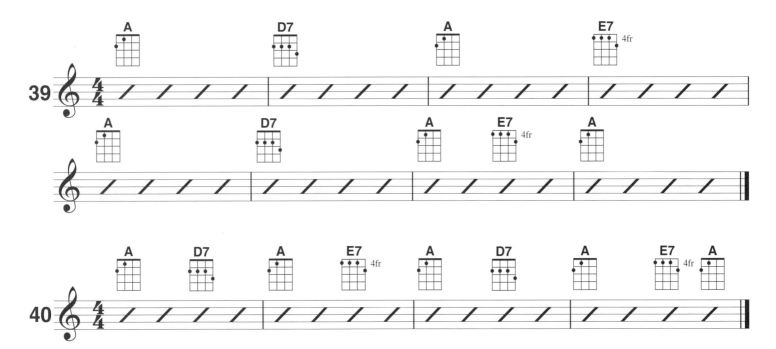

STRUM-ALONG TUNES IN A

Use the common (down, up, down, up) stroke on these tunes, putting the emphasis on the **backbeats** (2 and 4 of each measure). Listen to the recording, then try and play along.

HAND ME DOWN MY WALKING CANE

By James A. Bland

41
 A E7 4fr A D7

Hand me down my walking cane, hand me down my walking cane, hand me down my

 A E7 4fr A

walking cane, I'm leaving on the morning train. All my sins, they have overtaken me.

ROLLING IN MY SWEET BABY'S ARMS

Traditional

42
 A E7 4fr A A7

Rolling in my sweet baby's arms, I'll be rolling in my sweet baby's arms. Lay around that shack

 D7 A E7 4fr A

'til the mail train comes back. I'll be rolling in my sweet baby's arms.

THE OLD GRAY MARE

Traditional Folk

43
 A E7 4fr

The old gray mare, she ain't what she used to be, ain't what she used to be,

 A

ain't what she used to be. The old gray mare, she ain't what she used to be

 E7 4fr A D7 A D7 A

many long years ago. Many long years ago, many long years ago.

 E7 4fr A

The old gray mare, she ain't what she used to be, many long years ago.

Here's our first single-note reading melody in the key of A.

WORRIED MAN BLUES

Traditional Folk

1. It takes a wor-ried man to sing a wor-ried song. It
went a-cross the riv-er and I laid down to sleep. I

takes a wor-ried man to sing a wor-ried song. It
went a-cross the riv-er and I laid down to sleep. I

takes a wor-ried man to sing a wor-ried song. I'm wor-ried
went a-cross the riv-er and I laid down to sleep. When I woke

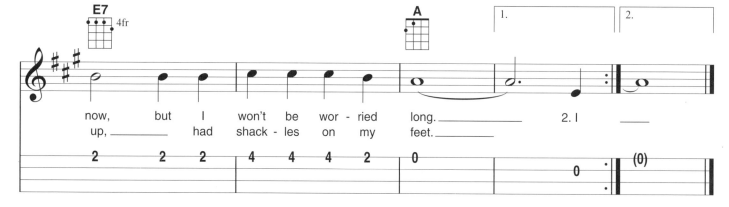

now, but I won't be wor-ried long._____ 2. I _____
up, _____ had shack-les on my feet._____

3. Twenty-one long links of chain around my leg. (3x)
   And on each link an initial of my name.

4. You know I asked that judge what's gonna be my fine. (3x)
   Ninety-nine years on the Rocky Mountain Line.

5. I looked down that road far as my eyes could see. (3x)
   Little bitty hand was waving after me.

Going up the neck will take a little practice and often requires the use of your fret-hand pinky.

HARD, AIN'T IT HARD

Traditional

3. The first time I saw my true love,
She was walking by my door,
The last time I saw her false-hearted smile,
Dead on the barroom floor.

BANKS OF THE OHIO

Traditional Ballad

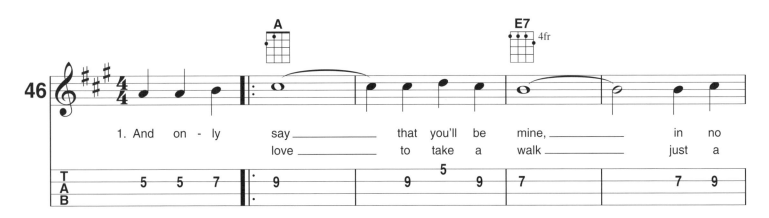

1. And on - ly say _____ that you'll be mine, _____ in no
love _____ to take a walk _____ just a

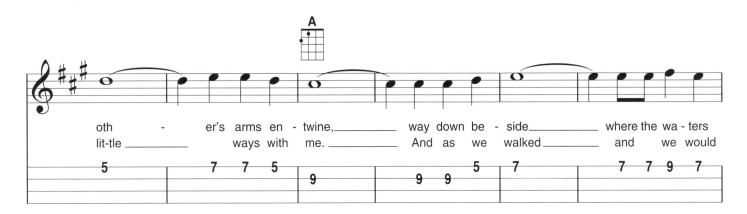

oth - er's arms en - twine, _____ way down be - side _____ where the wa - ters
lit-tle _____ ways with me. _____ And as we walked _____ and we would

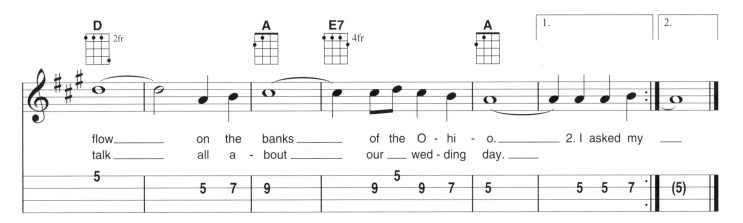

flow _____ on the banks _____ of the O - hi - o. _____ 2. I asked my _____
talk _____ all a - bout _____ our ___ wed - ding day. _____

3. I asked her if she'd marry me
And my wife forever be.
She only turned her head away
And had no other words to say.

4. I plunged a knife into her breast
And told her she was going to rest.
She cried, "Oh Willy, don't murder me.
I'm not prepared for eternity."

5. And going home between twelve and one,
I cried, "Lord, what have I done?"
I've killed the girl I love
Because she would not marry me.

HAMMER-ONS, PULL-OFFS, AND SLIDES

The next song, "Cripple Creek," will introduce you to three new techniques: the hammer-on, the pull-off, and the slide. These are called left-hand techniques since your left or fretting hand is the one that produces the desired effect. In all three techniques, the first note is voiced by picking in the normal way (with the right hand if you're right-handed). The second note is voiced by hammering on, pulling off, or sliding with the fretting hand.

HAMMER-ON

The arching **slur** from a lower note to a higher one in the music indicates a hammer-on. Voice the first note (fretted or open) by picking the string with your right hand. While that note is still ringing, hammer down on the next fret indicated with the appropriate finger of your left hand. The second note should sound without having to pick it with your right hand. Try this hammer-on exercise.

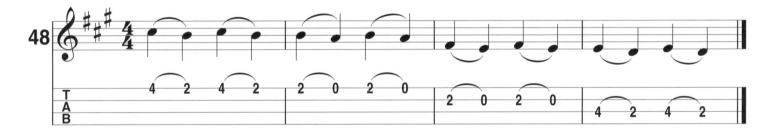

PULL-OFF

The slur from a higher note to a lower one indicates a pull-off. This is basically the reverse action of the hammer-on. First pluck a fretted note. While the note is still ringing, pull your left finger off the string with a plucking-type action. The second note should sound without having to be picked again. Try this pull-off exercise.

> **Tip**: When the second note is fretted and not open, make sure you're prepared by fretting that note with your next finger **before** you perform the pull-off.

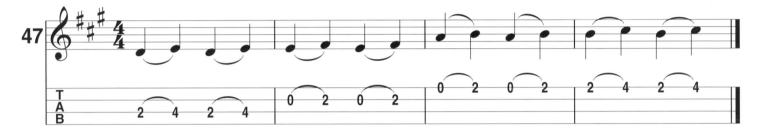

SLIDE

A straight slash from one note to another (sometimes with the letter "S" over it) indicates a slide. Slides are always from one fretted note to another. To perform a slide, first play a note in the normal way. While it is still ringing, slide the fretting finger to the fret indicated for the second note, all the while pressing down on the string. Though you don't have to squeeze hard, do not lift your finger or the sound will die. The second note will ring without having to pick it with your right hand. Try this exercise.

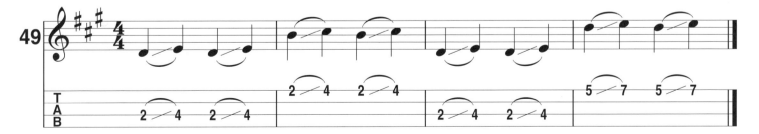

Now you're ready to play "Cripple Creek." This tune is played by every parking lot picker worth his or her salt!

CRIPPLE CREEK

Traditional Fiddle Tune

RAGTIME STRUM AND CHORD PATTERN

Using your strumming index finger:

Count 1 • strum *down*

Count 2 • strum *down*

Count & • quick strum *up*

Count 3 • rest

Count & • quick strum *up*

Count 4 • strum *down*

COUNT: **1** **2** **&** **3** **&** **4**

STRUM: ⊓ ⊓ V rest V ⊓

*(⊓)

* Optional downstroke on beat 3

The familiar ragtime chord pattern is I–VI–II–V–I in any key. For example, in the key of C you'd count up six letters to go from the I to the VI chord: C-D-E-F-G-A. The II chord in the key of C is D, and the V is G. All the chords (except the I) are dominant 7th chords, giving this progression a strong push to keep cycling around until it gets back to the I chord.

RAGTIME EXERCISES

Using the ragtime strum, let's learn this chord pattern in four of the most common keys: C, D, G, and F. Listen as I sometimes play a downstroke on beat 3 instead of a rest for variety.

RAGTIME HISTORY

Rag, which is short for ragtime, developed as a musical form in the early 1900s. Scott Joplin is widely regarded as its originator. While most of ragtime's early practitioners played the piano, it wasn't long before the style had influenced everything from blues, dixieland, and country, to Hawaiian music and later, rock 'n' roll. Popular songs with a ragtime influence include Arlo Guthrie's "Alice's Restaurant," the Beatles' "When I'm Sixty-Four," and Robert Johnson's "They're Red Hot." Classic ragtime numbers include "The Twelfth Street Rag," "Dill Pickles Rag," "The Tiger Rag," "The Entertainer," "Maple Leaf Rag," and "The Stones Rag (Stringband Rag)."

Now let's apply the ragtime ukulele strum and pattern to some songs. For measure 11 only of our first tune, use four down-strokes instead of the strum pattern. The I–VI–II–V–I progression starts in measure 9. Again, sometimes I strum on beat 3 instead of rest.

JUG BAND RAG

By Lil' Rev

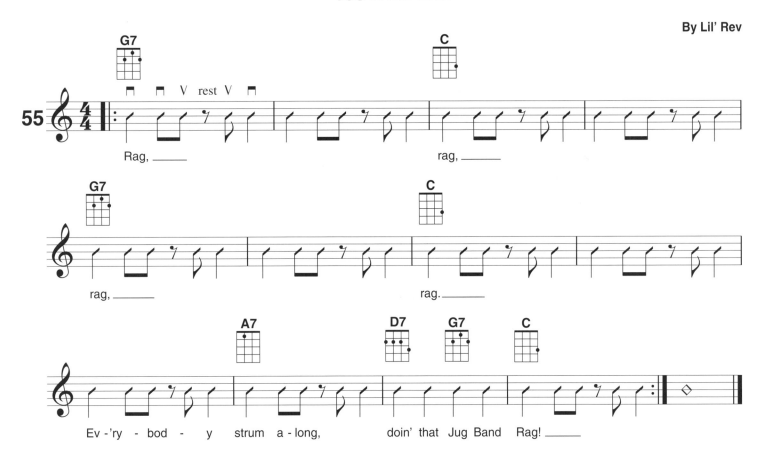

JUG BAND HISTORY

Jug band music grew up in the American South on the streets of cities like Memphis, Tennessee and Louisville, Kentucky. The music was derived from many different sources and was played on home-made instruments like the washboard, kazoo, and washtub bass. The Memphis Jug Band and Cannon's Jug Stompers were the two greatest bands in the tradition. Other important purveyors of jug band music include Clifford Hays, Jack Kelly's South Memphis Jug Band, and the Mississippi Sheiks (a string band).

Jug band music experienced a revival of interest in the 1960s with the arrival of groups like the Jim Kweskin Jug Band, Dave Van Ronk's Jug Stompers, and the Even Dozen Jug Band. Classic songs from the jug band era include "Stealing, Stealing," "Walk Right In," "KC Moan," "Going to Germany," "You May Leave," "Sadie Green," and "Boodle Am Shake," just to name a few.

In measure 9 of "Uke-in' the Rags," you'll meet another one of the most common chord progressions played on the ukulele: I–I7–IV–#IV♭7. Early jazz standards and Hawaiian music rely heavily on these kinds of patterns.

First, practice the down-down-up, up-down ragtime strum. Be ready to play only downstrokes in measures 3 and 15.

Next, slowly finger the C, A7, D7, and G7 chords, taking your time to name each chord as you strum. Work on switching chords smoothly, without any change in your steady timekeeping. Notice that measures 5–8 start off the same as 1–4. When those two phrases are solid, practice measures 9–12 as a separate phrase. Then hook up the phrases and play the whole song.

UKE-IN' THE RAGS

By Lil' Rev

THE FIVE-FINGER ROLL STROKE

The five-finger roll stroke is a great way to add punch and rhythm to your right-hand strumming. It emphasizes the downbeat of the strum by unraveling your right-hand fingers one by one, followed immediately thereafter by the thumb, in one continuous flowing stroke. Just like you imagined in the single-stroke roll, think of flicking a tiny ball of paper off a desk with one finger. Then imagine flicking four tiny balls of paper in one consecutive motion, ending with the thumb following right behind in one sweeping movement.

1. Start with your fingers curled in toward your palm.

2. Bring your right-hand pinky down across all four strings.

3. Let your third (ring) finger follow right after your pinky.

4. Now, your second (middle) finger follows down across all four strings.

5. Then your first (index) finger follows down across all four strings.

6. Finally, your thumb follows through all four strings, completing the roll stroke.

Here's the five-finger roll stroke in D major on "Shave and a Haircut."

Now play the five-finger roll stroke in A major.

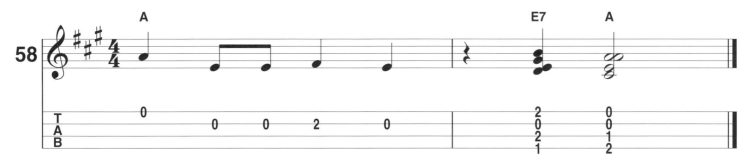

THE CALYPSO STRUM

This is a **syncopated** strum. Syncopation happens when we emphasize the "ands" of any given measure. This may be written by placing a rest on the beat, by tying eighth notes together, or by placing quarter notes on the off beats. While playing this rhythm may feel awkward at first, once you have this pattern down, you'll find it to be infectious! Then look up some other calypso tunes like "Day-O," "Maryanne," "All My Trials," or "Jamaica Farewell."

To learn the strum, first try dampening the strings with your left hand and concentrating on the pattern with your right hand only. Count steady 4/4 time aloud. On beat 3, let your hand miss the strings as it makes a downstroke.

COUNT: **1   2   &   3   &   4   &**
STRUM: down down up (miss) up down up

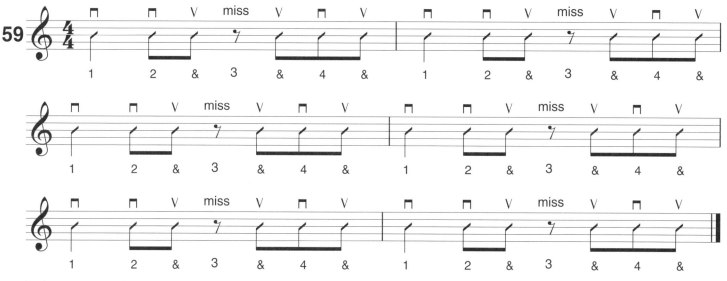

Let's start out with some very easy chords.

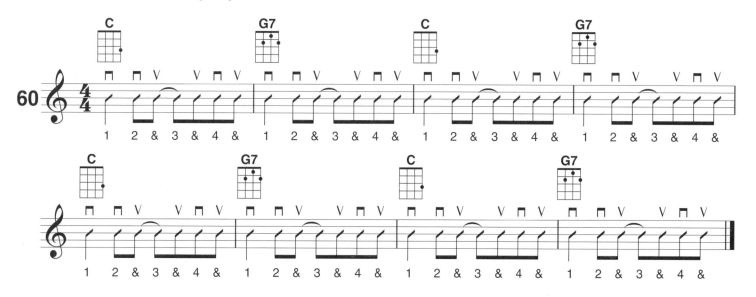

Now let's try the calypso strum with something a little harder.

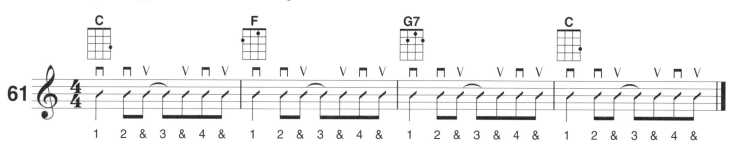

33

This is a great, catchy little calypso melody. Practice the melody slowly at first, gradually working it up to a medium tempo.

PAY ME MY MONEY DOWN

By Lillian Parrish
Arranged by Lil' Rev

3. I thought I heard the old man say, pay me my money down,
   Go to shore, spend all your pay, pay me my money down.

With this next arrangement we'll focus on playing the strum and singing the tune. After each of the three verses, sing the chorus, for a total of six times through the chord progression.

SLOOP JOHN B.

Caribbean Folk

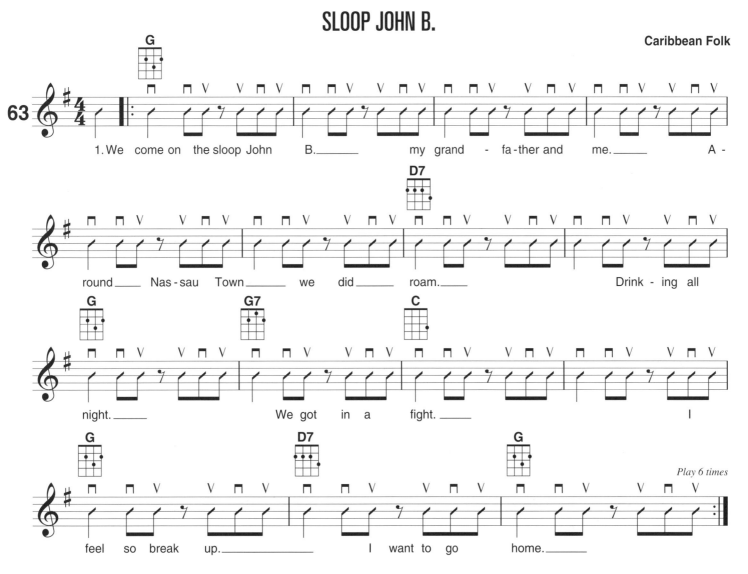

Chorus: So, hoist up the John B. sails. See how the main sail sets. Call for the captain ashore, let me go home.
I want to go home, well, I want to go home. I feel so break up, well, I want to go home.

2. Well, the poor cook, he got fits, threw away all the grits. Then he went, ate up all of my corn.
Sheriff John Stome, well, let me go home. I feel so break up, well, I want to go home.

3. Well, the first mate, he got drunk, threw away the people's trunk. Then he went, ate up all of my corn.
Let me go home, let me go home. I feel so break up, well, I want to go home.

CALYPSO HISTORY

Having developed in Trinidad over 100 years ago, calypso encompasses folk music from the Bahamas, Jamaica, and the surrounding Caribbean islands. The calypso repertoire, much like early blues, uses syncopated beats and simple chord structures in its composition, as well as *double entendre* in its lyrics. The influence of calypso music can be traced back through a diverse array of talented artists like Blind Blake, the Jolly Boys, Calypso Mama, Andre Toussaint, and George Symonette.

While calypso has been a part of Caribbean culture for as long as we can remember, it wasn't until the late 1950s and early sixties that it began to grow in popularity here in America, when singers like Harry Belafonte, Nina Simone, and the Weavers all began to use calypso as a regular part of their shows. It should be noted that, in 1956, Harry Belafonte turned calypso into an overnight sensation with his renditions of "Day-O" and "Jamaica Farewell." Belafonte's calypso record became the first album in history to sell one million copies—outselling even Elvis Presley at the time.

PLAYING THE BOOGIE-WOOGIE

The boogie-woogie originated in the barrooms, juke joints, and speakeasies of the early to mid-1900s. Often associated with blues and jazz piano and bass guitar, the boogie-woogie has influenced every style of American music from country-western to blues, rock, and more. In the following exercise, we will explore playing boogie-woogie in the key of G, a key that works well on the ukulele, as we can take advantage of the open strings. As with every exercise, start slowly and gradually build up your speed. The boogie-woogie can be played as either accompaniment to most 12-bar blues song forms or as a solo.

This boogie-woogie pattern will require the use of all four fretting fingers on your left hand, so it's a great exercise in dexterity, as well as good practice reading and playing eighth notes. Use your thumb to pick these series of eighth notes. Drive cautiously, now!

THE SHUFFLE

In traditional styles like blues and jazz, eighth notes are played unevenly. Play the first note twice as long as the second.

Playing the eighth notes in this way will give you the desired shuffle or "swing" feel, as played in the following song.

UKE BOOGIE IN G

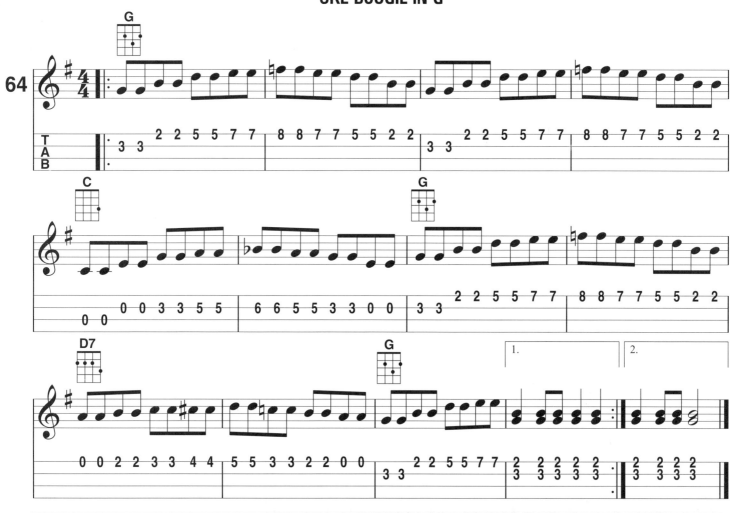

BOOGIE-WOOGIE CLASSICS

There are hundreds of classic boogie-woogie tunes that you should be able to track down. Here are a few of my favorites: "Red Hot," "Tear It Up," "You Don't Know My Mind," "Blue Suede Shoes," "Big Walter's Boogie," and "Good Morning Blues"—to name a few! It is important to spend time absorbing the classics. Listen to the works of Leadbelly, Elvis, Chuck Berry, Otis Spann, Memphis Slim, Little Walter, Bill Haley and the Comets, and John Lee Hooker.

THE TRIPLET STROKE

The triplet stroke is one of the most common and distinctive ukulele strums. While there are numerous ways to execute this highly rhythmic stroke, the easiest way is as follows:

1. With a downstroke, bring your first finger down across all four strings.

2. Just as your first finger completes its brush across all four strings, let your thumb follow down across all four strings.

3. As your thumb leaves the last string (A), bring your first finger quickly back up across all four strings.

The emphasis (accent) is on the first beat, so the first finger downstroke should be hard and the following down and up strokes a little lighter.

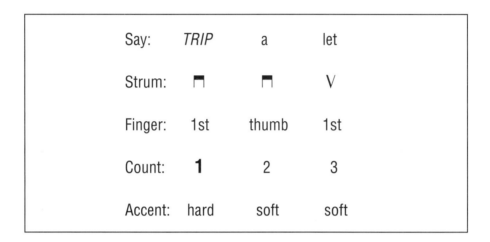

Say:	*TRIP*	a	let
Strum:	⊓	⊓	V
Finger:	1st	thumb	1st
Count:	**1**	2	3
Accent:	hard	soft	soft

Once you start to get the hang of this, gradually begin to increase your speed. Think of a train leaving the station—slowly, then gradually increasing its momentum. At this point, you will have a steady triplet rhythm, unbroken by irregular beats.

TRIPLETS AND 6/8 TIME

If a song in 4/4 time has only a few triplets here and there, then the time signature does not change. Instead, the triplets are marked with a little number "3" that implies "three in the space usually taken by two." The three beamed notes take one beat, or one foot-tap on the floor.

When triplet rhythms are used consistently throughout a song, it is more-easily written and read in 6/8 time. Each measure has two main accented beats.

This basic blues progression in 6/8 time is a great way to practice your triplet stroke. Start slowly and try to keep an even pace.

TRIPLET STROKE BLUES

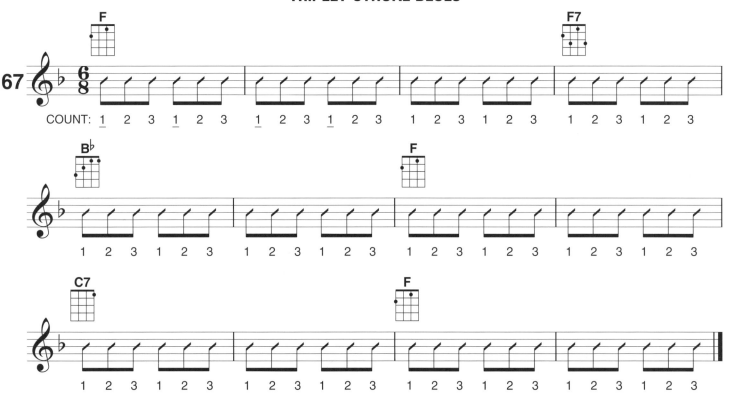

COUNT: <u>1</u> 2 3 <u>1</u> 2 3 <u>1</u> 2 3 <u>1</u> 2 3 1 2 3 1 2 3 1 2 3 1 2 3

1 2 3 1 2 3 1 2 3 1 2 3 1 2 3 1 2 3 1 2 3 1 2 3

1 2 3 1 2 3 1 2 3 1 2 3 1 2 3 1 2 3 1 2 3 1 2 3

TRIPLET EXERCISES

Try the triplet stroke with this basic chord progression.

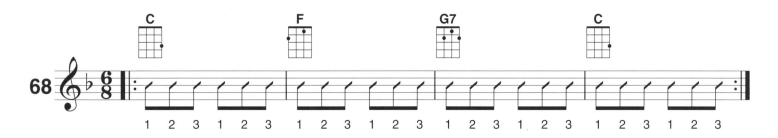

1 2 3 1 2 3 1 2 3 1 2 3 1 2 3 1 2 3 1 2 3 1 2 3

Great! Now let's spice it up a bit!

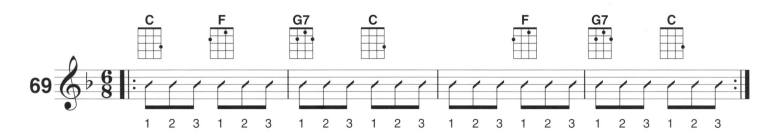

1 2 3 1 2 3 1 2 3 1 2 3 1 2 3 1 2 3 1 2 3 1 2 3

Here are two basic chord progressions for the triplet strum. Practice these until you build up some speed.

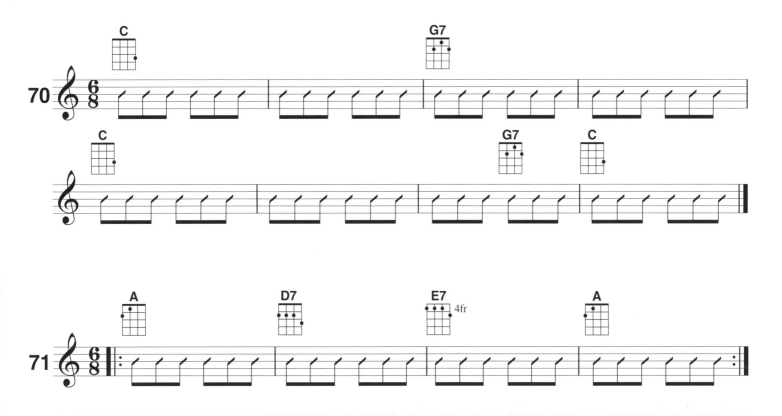

THE SHUFFLE REVISITED

If the second attack of a triplet is skipped, you get the shuffle rhythm. If the second and third attack of a triplet are skipped, you get what sounds like a regular quarter note (meas. 2 and 3). The dot indicates that the quarter note is now three eighth notes long, insuring the measure fits the new time signature. Slowly count and play these rhythms.

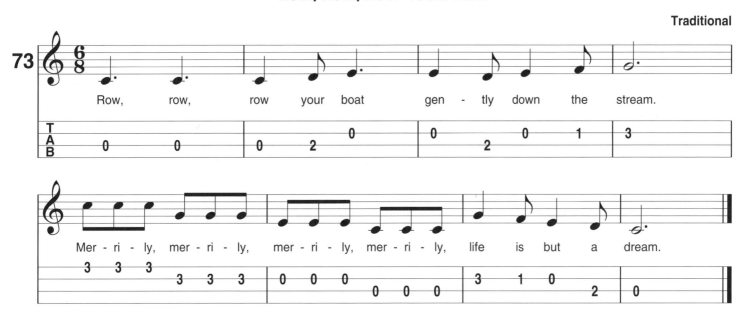

Now try some melodies in 6/8 time.

ROW, ROW, ROW YOUR BOAT

Traditional

THREE BLIND MICE

Traditional

Three blind mice, three blind mice.

See how they run, see how they run._____ They all ran af-ter the farm-er's wife who cut off their tails with a carv-ing knife. Did you ev-er see such a sight in your life as three blind mice.

Listening to Irish music will give you a great feel for the 6/8 time signature. Some of my favorites include "The Swallow Tail Jig," "The Road to Lisdonvarna," "Lanigan's Ball," "All for Me Grog," and "The Irish Washerwoman" (in this book!).

POP GOES THE WEASEL

Traditional Jig

Half_____ a pound of tup-pen-ney rice, half_____ a pound of trea - cle. That's_____ the way the mon - ey goes, pop goes the wea - sel. Half__ wea - sel.

Here's a very popular Irish jig you may have heard before. Start playing this piece slowly at first, gradually building up speed until you can play it fast. Parts A and B are each played twice. This song form is common in fiddle tunes and is often referred to as AABB.

Concentrate on using your thumb to pick these melody notes. When you can play it at moderate speed, you will feel a great sense of accomplishment. If it's too hard for you to play it up to speed with your thumb, you may want to try this one using a pick.

THE IRISH WASHERWOMAN

Irish Folksong

Here's one more song in 6/8 for good measure.

I'SE THE B'Y THAT BUILDS THE BOAT

Canadian Folk Song
Arranged by Lil' Rev

MORE IN 3/4

As discussed earlier, in the 3/4 time signature (also called *waltz* time), we count 1-2-3, 1-2-3, or oom-pah-pah, oom-pah-pah. The note values in each measure must always add up to three beats. Let's begin with a classic! Play this in "turtle time" (really slow).

HOME ON THE RANGE

Traditional

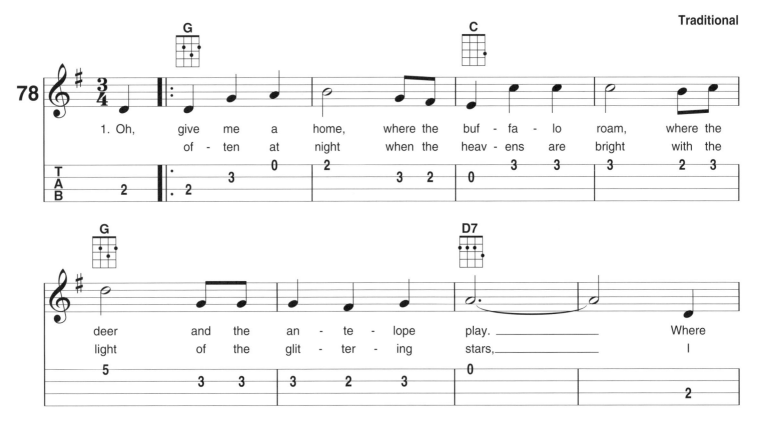

Here's a simple folk tune in the familiar key of G.

BEAUTIFUL BROWN EYES

Traditional

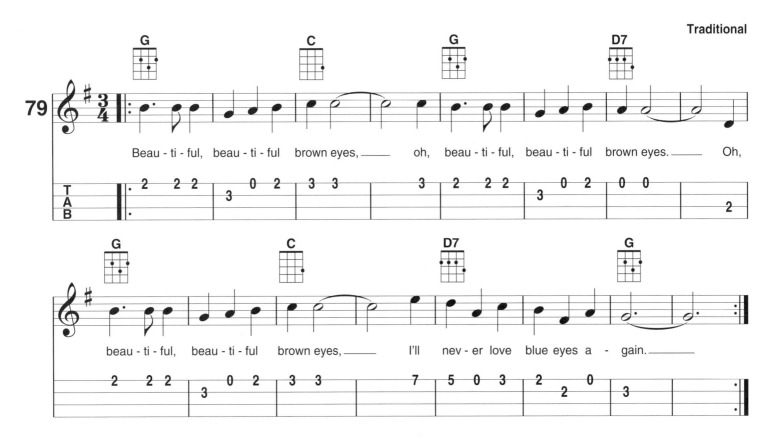

Note the pull-off in the second full measure of this tune in D.

RYE WHISKEY

Traditional

WORKING IN MINOR KEYS

In *Ukulele Method Book 1*, we introduced you to the keys of E minor and D minor. Now let's revisit those keys and then add a couple of new ones: G minor and A minor.

This exercise is in D minor. Start out slow and eventually work it up to a faster pace.

1937 SWING

By Lil' Rev

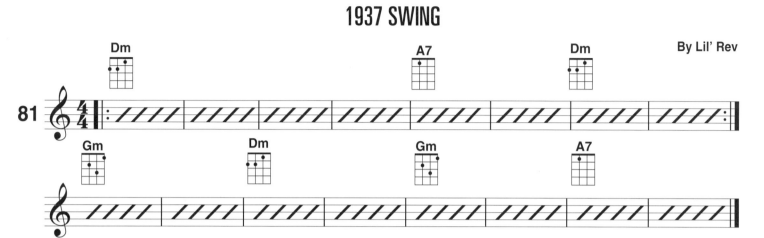

Changing chords multiple times within the space of one measure should be getting easier now! This one is in E minor.

GOIN' MINOR

(à la St. James Infirmary)

By Lil' Rev

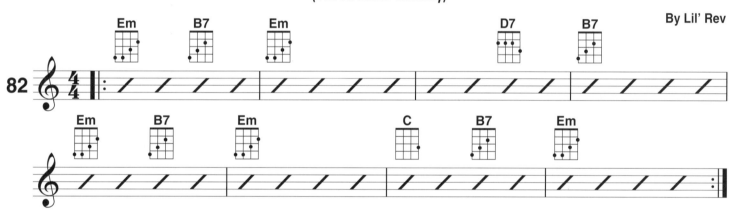

Take this one slowly. It contains five new chord shapes and is in the key of G minor. We also get some minor seventh chords here. Minor 7th chords are spelled $1\text{–}\flat3\text{–}5\text{–}\flat7$ from the root of the chord. For example, Gm7 contains the notes G–B$\flat$–D–F. Say the chord names out loud as you practice them.

ALL THE WAY MINOR

By Lil' Rev

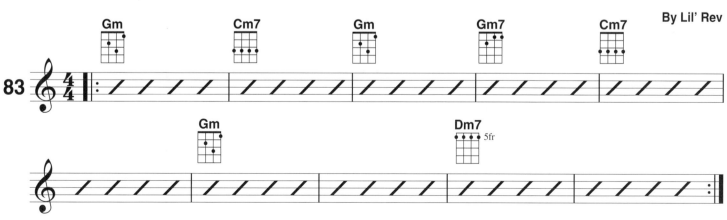

DRUNKEN SAILOR

Traditional Sea Song

3. Rub his belly with a rusty razor. (2x)
   Rub his belly with a rusty razor early in the morning.

4. Show him the Bible and he'll find Jesus. (2x)
   Show him the Bible and he'll find Jesus early in the morning.

5. Put him in the scuppers with a hosepipe in him. (2x)
   Put him in the scuppers with a hosepipe in him early in the morning.

GREENSLEEVES
(Single-String Lead Version)

Old English Folk

UKULELE RESOURCES

History Books

Beloff, Jim. *Ukulele: A Visual History*. Miller Freeman/Hal Leonard.

Ewen, David. *The Life and Death of Tin Pan Alley*. Funk and Wagnalls.

Furia, Phillip. *The Poets of Tin Pan Alley*. Oxford University Press.

Snyder, Robert W. *The Voice of the City: Vaudeville and Pop Culture in New York City*. Ivan R Dee.

Whitcomb, Ian. *After the Ball*. Penguin Books.

Songbooks

Beloff, Jim. *Jumpin' Jim's Ukulele Gems*. Hal Leonard.

Beloff, Jim. *Jumpin' Jim's Ukulele Favorites*. Hal Leonard.

Beloff, Jim and Ohta, Herb. *Jumpin' Jim's Ukulele Masters: Herb Ohta: Sophisticated Ukulele*. Hal Leonard.

Beloff, Jim and Ritz, Lyle. *Jumpin' Jim's Ukulele Masters: Lyle Ritz: Jazz*. Hal Leonard.

Formby, George. *George Formby Songbook*. Wise Publications.

Middlebrook, Ron. *Ukulele Songbook*. Centerstream/Hal Leonard.

Web Sites

Elderly Instruments (recordings, books and instruments). www.elderly.com.

Jumpin' Jim's (instruments, books and all things uke). www.fleamarketmusic.com.

Ukulele Boogaloo—All things uke. www.alligatorboogaloo.com.

Ukulele Hall of Fame and Museum. www.ukulele.org.

Ukulelia—a great uke blog. www.ukulelia.com.